Rookie
Read-About® Geography

Alabama

By Holli Leber

Consultant
Nanci R. Vargus, Ed.D.
Assistant Professor of Literacy
University of Indianapolis
Indianapolis, Indiana

Children's Press®
A Division of Scholastic Inc.
New York   Toronto   London   Auckland   Sydney
Mexico City   New Delhi   Hong Kong
Danbury, Connecticut

Designer: Herman Adler Design
Photo Researcher: Caroline Anderson
The photo on the cover shows Bellingrath Gardens and Home in
Theodore, Alabama.

Library of Congress Cataloging-in-Publication Data

Leber, Holli.
  Alabama / by Holli Leber.
      p. cm. — (Rookie read-about geography)
Includes index.
Summary: A simple introduction to Alabama, focusing on its regions and
their geographical features.
  ISBN 0-516-22719-X (lib. bdg.)   0-516-27945-9 (pbk.)
  1. Alabama—Juvenile literature. 2. Alabama—Geography—Juvenile
literature. [1. Alabama.] I. Title. II. Series.
  F326.3.L43 2004
  917.6'1—dc22
                                        2003016891

CHILDREN'S PRESS, and ROOKIE READ-ABOUT®,
and associated logos are trademarks and or registered trademarks
of Scholastic Library Publishing. SCHOLASTIC and associated logos
are trademarks and or registered trademarks of Scholastic Inc.

1 2 3 4 5 6 7 8 9 10 R 13 12 11 10 09 08 07 06 05 04

Do you know why Alabama
is called the Heart of Dixie?

Dixie is a nickname for
the southeastern part of the
United States.

Alabama is right at the heart,
or middle, of this part.

Can you find Alabama on
this map?

CANADA

WASHINGTON
OREGON
IDAHO
MONTANA
NORTH DAKOTA
SOUTH DAKOTA
WYOMING
MINNESOTA
WISCONSIN
MICHIGAN
NEW HAMPSHIRE
VERMONT
MAINE
NEVADA
UTAH
COLORADO
NEBRASKA
IOWA
ILLINOIS
INDIANA
OHIO
NEW YORK
MASSACHUSETTS
RHODE ISLAND
CONNECTICUT
NEW JERSEY
PENNSYLVANIA
WEST VIRGINIA
DELAWARE
MARYLAND
CALIFORNIA
ARIZONA
NEW MEXICO
KANSAS
MISSOURI
KENTUCKY
VIRGINIA
Washington, D.C.
OKLAHOMA
ARKANSAS
TENNESSEE
NORTH CAROLINA
SOUTH CAROLINA
ALABAMA
GEORGIA
TEXAS
MISSISSIPPI
LOUISIANA
FLORIDA

North
West   East
South

ALASKA   CANADA
MEXICO
HAWAII

5

In Alabama, shrubs and trees bloom in the spring. The state flower is the camellia.

The state bird is the yellowhammer.

There are mountains
and streams in northern
Alabama. The land is hilly
and covered with forests.

The soil is red because
it has iron in it.

Part of northern Alabama
is called the Appalachian
Highlands.

Coal, limestone, and marble
can be found under the
hills there.

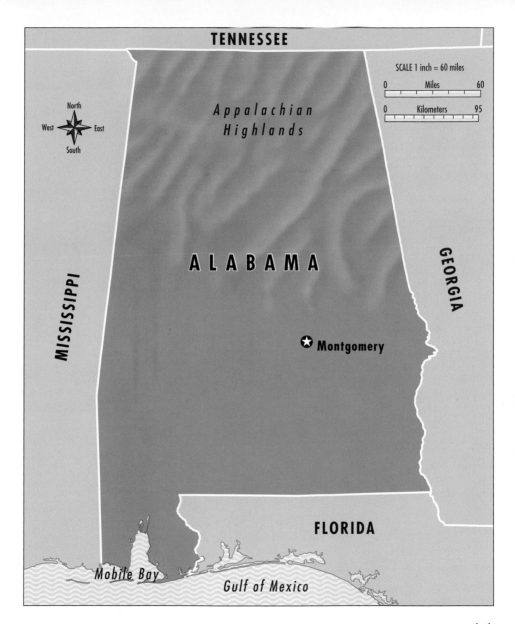

12

The Piedmonts are south of the Highlands. These low hills are covered with trees.

Cheaha Mountain is the highest spot in Alabama.

The Black Belt crosses
the middle of Alabama.
This strip of land is named
for its sticky black soil.

In the past, cotton was
the main crop in Alabama.
It was grown in the
Black Belt.

Cattle

Farmers still grow cotton in the Black Belt. They grow corn, peanuts, and soybeans, too.

They also raise cattle, chickens, and hogs.

Pine forests cover part of
the Gulf Coastal Plain.
A plain is flat land.

The state tree is the
longleaf pine.

The rest of the Gulf Coastal Plain has swamps. A swamp is wet, spongy land.

Alligators and other animals live in the swamps.

The southern tip of Alabama is shaped like a boot heel. The heel is split in two by Mobile Bay.

Fishing and shipping are important jobs in this part of Alabama.

Birmingham is the largest
city in Alabama. More steel
comes from Birmingham
than any other city in
the South.

Capitol building in Montgomery

Montgomery is the
state capital.

Huntsville is another large city in Alabama. The U.S. Space and Rocket Center is there.

Children visit the center
to learn what it is like to
be an astronaut.

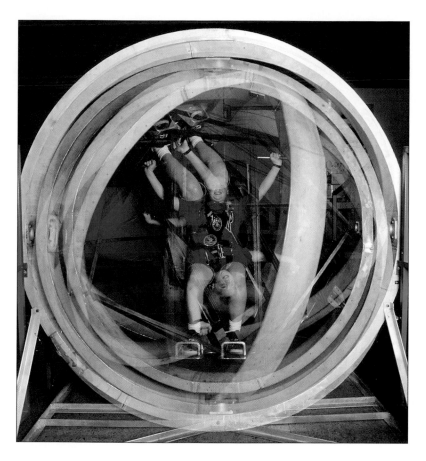

Maybe you will visit
Alabama one day.

What part would you
most like to see?

Words You Know

alligator

camellia

Cheaha Mountain

cotton

30

longleaf pine tree

steel

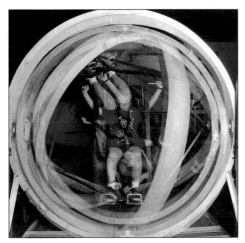

U.S. Space and Rocket
Center

yellowhammer

31

Index

About the Author

Holli Leber is a freelance writer. She has a Bachelor of Arts degree from Skidmore College. She lives in Saratoga Springs, New York.

Photo Credits

Photographs © 2004: Corbis Images/Bill Varie: 9; Dembinsky Photo Assoc.: 19, 20, 30 top left, 31 top left (Bill Lea), 6, 30 top right (Richard Shiell); ImageState/ Andre Jenny: 25; Milton Fullman: 12, 15, 23, 30 bottom right, 30 bottom left; The Image Works: 26, 27, 31 bottom left (Michael J. Doolittle), 24, 31 top right (Karim Shamsi-Basha); Unicorn Stock Photos: 7, 31 bottom right (Robert E. Barber), 16 (Jeff Greenberg), 3 (Chuck Schmeiser), 8 (Dennis Thompson); William H. Allen: cover, 29.

Maps by Bob Italiano